A Crash in the Night

Mary Ann Steiner, Sam Taylor, and Judy Diamond

Illustrations by Mary Ann Steiner

Zea Books
Lincoln, Nebraska

ISBN 978-1-609-62-151-3

doi 10.32873/unl.dc.zea.1075

Set in Myriad types.

Zea Books are published by the University of Nebraska-Lincoln Libraries.

Nebraska
UNIVERSITY OF
Lincoln

To Our Readers

The illustrations in this book describe a wildlife encounter. Wild animals, like people, have challenges in life. They are adaptable and inventive, and they find new ways of solving problems to help them survive. As you turn the pages, describe what you see. How would you solve this wildlife challenge?

Fox

Coyote

Wolf

Dog

16

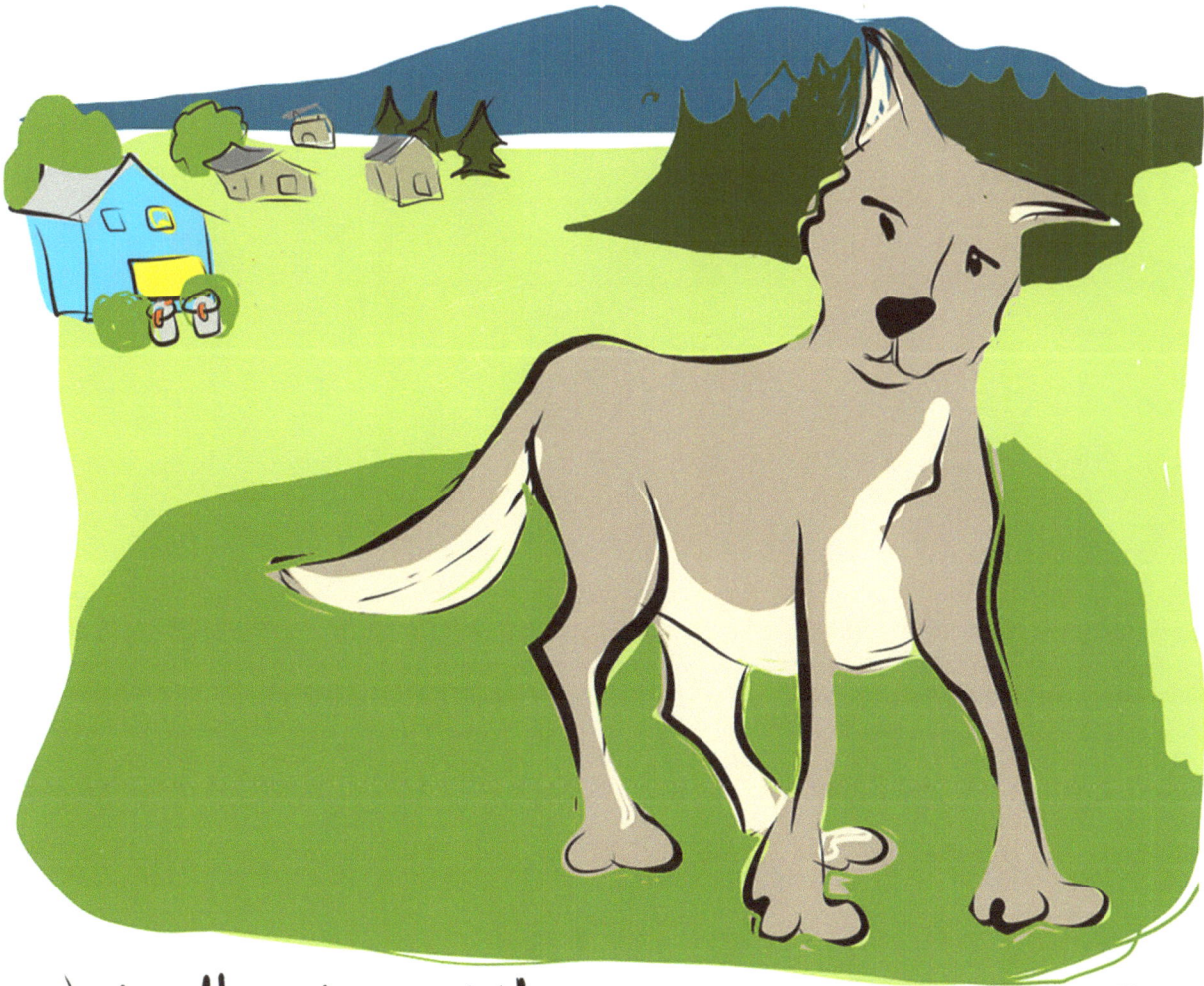

What will coyote do now?

The End

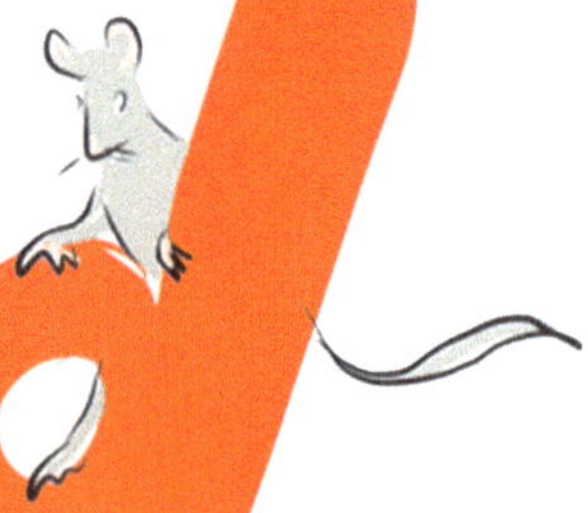

Notes from the authors

Mary Ann Steiner: Working on this story was exciting to me because I believe at any age, we can notice what is happening around us and make decisions to protect and enjoy nature! In this story, the kids see an exciting new character in the community. Once they figure out who it is, they look to understand more about the coyote. Sure, coyotes could eat a pet, but more often they are eating other wild animals like mice. If we can do things to make our yards less interesting to coyotes (and mice), they'd likely stay at a distance where we can listen to them and occasionally see them in action. This story connects curiosity, creativity, and enjoyment and respect for our role in nature.

Sam Taylor: What are the different ways to know nature? In my own experience as a marine biology researcher and museum director, I know there are many ways to connect with nature: whether through a scientific process or through personal experience. I grew up in Montana, but I was entranced by the ocean – stories about Jacques Cousteau and family vacations to Vancouver Island led me to want to discover as much as I could about the natural world. And then books gave me a portal to worlds both familiar and exotic and the realization that discovery and understanding can happen in settings as familiar as my backyard or as remote as the open seas.

Judy Diamond: I work in a natural history museum and study the behavior of animals like coyotes. I watch them in the wild to learn how they share and learn things. How do young coyotes learn to hunt? Do their parents teach them? Why do coyotes play? When they play, do they also learn how to get along with each other? Maybe playing helps them not fight so much. Coyotes are wonderful animals to study because they are very flexible. If one kind of food is not available, they can find others, since they eat plants and other animals. Coyotes can live in all sorts of places, even in large cities. They are champions at being adaptable. Just like people.

Coyote at Ridgefield National Wildlife Refuge, Washington
(Rebecca Richardson, CC-BY)

www.ingramcontent.com/pod-product-compliance
Lightning Source LLC
Chambersburg PA
CBHW060819270326

41930CB00002B/91